D1621158

3 0012 00247326 1

SONGS FROM
DEEP WATERS

Selections from the Psalms with prayer meditations

©Copyright Scandinavia Publishing House
Nørregade 32
DK 1165 Copenhagen K.
Denmark
Tel. 01-140091

©Text: Marlee Alex

Quotations from *The Holy Bible, New International Version*, copyright © 1978 by New York International Bible Society. Used by permission.

Printed in Singapore by TWP.

ISBN 87 7247 039 9

SONGS FROM DEEP WATERS

Selections from the Psalms with prayer meditations

Edited by Jørgen Vium Olesen
Text by Marlee Alex
Scripture text from The Holy Bible, New International Version

Scandinavia

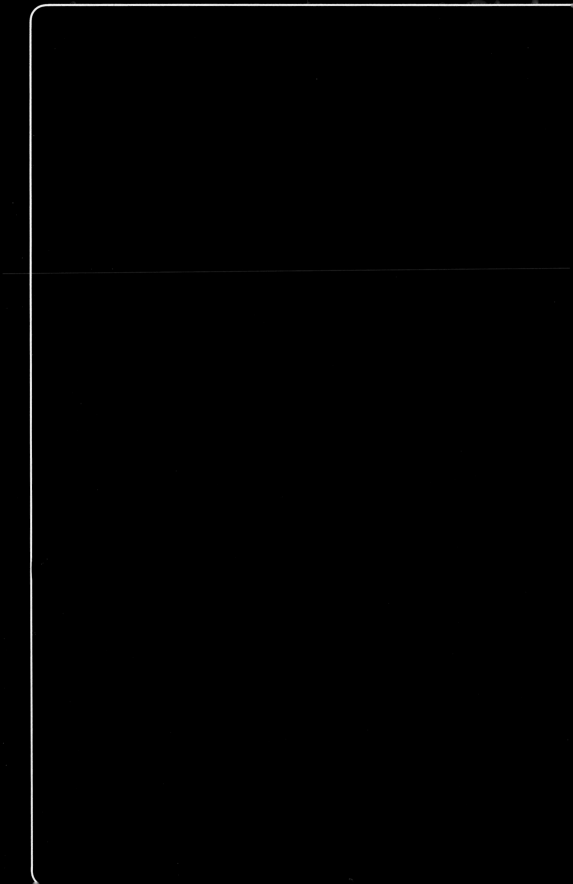

Send forth your
light and your truth,
let them guide me; let them
bring me to your holy
mountain, to the place
where you dwell.
Ps 43:3-4

Let me hear joy and gladness;
let the bones you have crushed rejoice.
Hide your face from my sins
and blot out all my iniquity.
Create in me a pure heart, O God,
and renew a steadfast spirit within me.
Do not cast me from your presence
or take your Holy Spirit from me.
Restore to me the joy of your salvation
and grant me a willing spirit, to sustain me.
Then I will teach transgressors your ways,
and sinners will turn back to you.
Save me from bloodguiltiness, O God,
the God who saves me, and my tongue will sing
of your righteousness. O Lord, open my lips,
and my mouth will declare your praise.
Ps.51:8-15

Abide in the Lord

Then I said, »Here I am, I have come — it is written about me in the scroll. I desire to do your will, O my God.«

I waited patiently for the Lord; he turned to me and heard my cry.
He lifted me out of the slimy pit, out of the mud and mire; he set my feet on a rock and gave me a firm place to stand.
He put a new song in my mouth, a hymn of praise to our God. Many will see and fear and put their trust in the Lord.
Blessed is the man who makes the Lord his trust, who does not look to the proud, to those who turn aside to false gods.
Many, O Lord my God, are the wonders you have done. The things you planned for us no one can recount to you; were I to speak and tell of them, they would be too many to declare.
Sacrifice and offering you did not desire, but my ears you have pierced; burnt offerings and sin offerings you did not require.
Then I said, »Here I am, I have come — it is written about me in the scroll.
I desire to do your will, O my God; your law is within my heart.«
I proclaim righteousness in the great assembly; I do not seal my lips, as you know, O Lord.
I do not hide your righteousness in my heart; I speak of your faithfulness and salvation. I do not conceal your love and your truth from the great assembly.
Do not withhold your mercy from me, O Lord; may your love and your truth always protect me.
For troubles without number surround me; my sins have overtaken me, and I cannot see. They are more than the hairs of my head, and my heart fails within me.
Be pleased, O Lord, to save me; O Lord, come quickly to help me.
May all who seek to take my life be put to shame and confusion; may all who desire my ruin be turned back in disgrace.
May those who say to me, »Aha! Aha!« be appalled at their own shame.
But may all who seek you rejoice and be glad in you; may those who love your salvation always say, »The Lord be exalted!«
Yet I am poor and needy; may the Lord think of me. You are my help and my deliverer; O my God, do not delay.

Be magnified through me, Lord, like a stream
gaining power as it rushes downward, like a
river growing broader as it surges onward, like
an open sea with no boundaries in view.

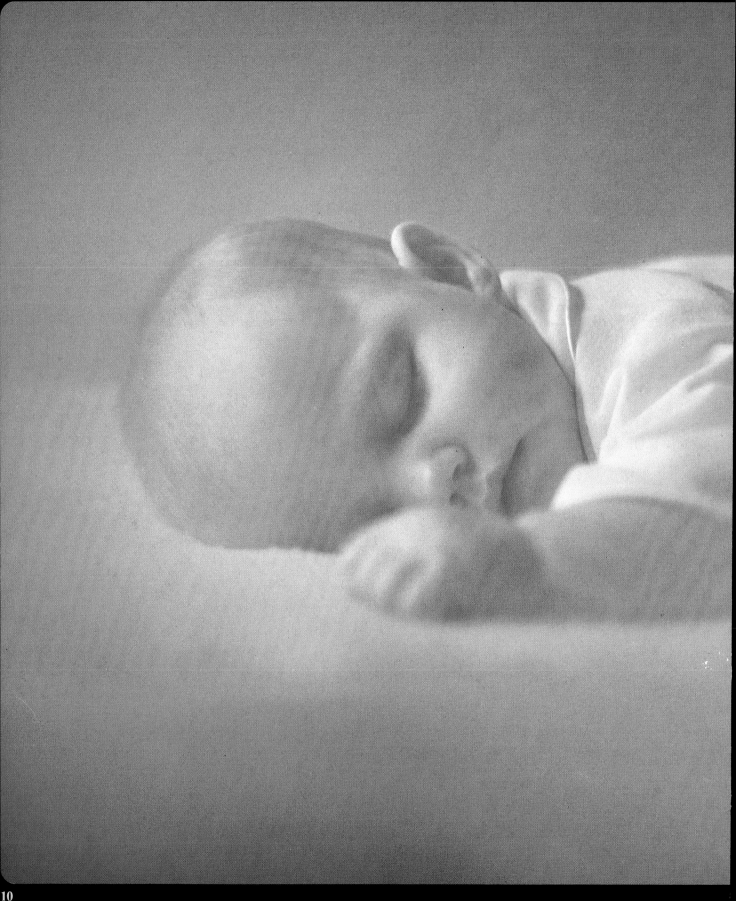

Trusting the Lord

Blessed is he who has regard for the weak; the
Lord delivers him in times of trouble.

Blessed is he who has regard for the weak; the Lord
delivers him in times of trouble.
The Lord will protect him and preserve his life; he will
bless him in the land and not surrender him to the desire
of his foes.
The Lord will sustain him on his sickbed and restore him
from his bed of illness.
I said, »O Lord, have mercy on me; heal me, for I have
sinned against you.«
My enemies say of me in malice, »When will he die and
his name perish?«
Whenever one comes to see me, he speaks falsely, while
his heart gathers slander; then he goes out and spreads it
abroad.
All my enemies whisper together against me; they
imagine the worst for me, saying,
»A vile disease has beset him; he will never get up from
the place where he lies.«
Even my close friend, whom I trusted, he who shared
my bread, has lifted up his heel against me.
But you, O Lord, have mercy on me; raise me up, that I
may repay them.
I know that you are pleased with me, for my enemy does
not triumph over me.
In my integrity you uphold me and set me in your
presence forever.
Praise be to the Lord, the God of Israel, from
everlasting to everlasting.
Amen and Amen

Lord, your heart is knitted to needs. You expect
that your people will »catch« your compassion
and follow suit. »Blessed are those who consider
the poor.« Caring for those who cannot care for
themselves is to be at one with the heart of God.

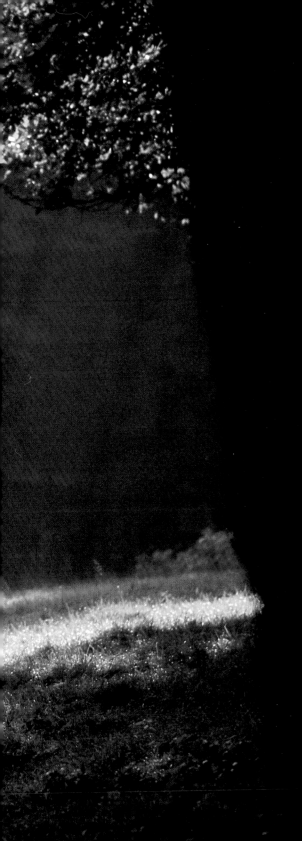

Thirst for God

*Why are you downcast, O my soul? Why so
disturbed within me? Put your hope in God, for I
will yet praise him, my Savior and my God.*

As the deer pants for streams of water, so my soul pants
for you, O God.
My soul thirsts for God, for the living God. When can I
go and meet with God?
My tears have been my food day and night, while men
say to me all day long, »Where is your God?«
These things I remember as I pour out my soul: how I
used to go with the multitude, leading the procession to
the house of God, with shouts of joy and thanksgiving
among the festive throng.

Why are you downcast, O my soul? Why so disturbed
within me? Put your hope in God, for I will yet praise
him, my Savior and my God.

My soul is downcast within me; therefore I will
remember you from the land of the Jordan, the heights
of Hermon — from Mount Mizar.
Deep calls to deep in the roar of your waterfalls; all your
waves and breakers have swept over me.

By day the Lord directs his love, at night his song is with
me — a prayer to the God of my life.
I say to God my Rock, »Why have you forgotten me?
Why must I go about mourning, oppressed by the
enemy?«
My bones suffer mortal agony as my foes taunt me,
saying to me all day long, »Where is your God?«

Why are you downcast, O my soul? Why so disturbed
within me? Put your hope in God, for I will yet praise
him, my savior and my God.

*My soul is like a darkened room, like a dense
forest, like murky waters. I'm alone, I'm
nervous, I'm suspicious. Yet, in the depths of
my mourning I faintly hear a song being sung. I
recognize your voice. The song becomes my
prayer. It gives me hope.*

God My Stronghold

Then will I go to the altar of God, to God, my joy and my delight.

Vindicate me, O God, and plead my cause against an ungodly nation; rescue me from deceitful and wicked men.
You are God my stronghold. Why have you rejected me? Why must I go about mourning, oppressed by the enemy?
Send forth your light and your truth, let them bring me to your holy mountain, to the place where you dwell.
Then will I go to the altar of God, to God, my joy and my delight. I will praise you with the harp, O God, my God.
Why are you downcast, O my soul? Why so disturbed within me? Put your hope in God, for I will yet praise him, my Savior and my God.

Your light and truth do not change my circumstances. They merely expose them for what they really are: opportunities in disguise, favorable chances for me to experience your power, latent possibilities for my growth and your glory.

The Victory Comes From the Lord

In God we make our boast all day long, and we will praise your name forever.

We have heard with our ears, O God; our fathers have told us what you did in their days, in days long ago.
With your hand you drove out the nations and planted our fathers; you crushed the peoples and made our fathers flourish.
It was not by their sword that they won the land, nor did their arm bring them victory; it was your right hand, your arm, and the light of your face, for you loved them.
You are my King and my God, who decrees victories for Jacob.
Through you we push back our enemies; through your name we trample our foes.
I do not trust in my bow, my sword does not bring me victory;
but you give us victory over our enemies, you put our adversaries to shame.
In God we make our boast all day long, and we will praise your name forever.

We have as our heritage the history of a people who followed God. The history continues. It is his story. And it convinces us that he is the farmer, the captian, the King. He plants and harvests from our land, fights our battles, and he reigns among us!

Rise Up and Help Us!

We are brought down to the dust; our bodies cling to the ground. Rise up and help us; redeem us because of your unfailing love.

But now your have rejected and humbled us; you no longer go out with our armies.
You made us retreat before the enemy, and our adversaries have plundered us.
You gave us up to be devoured like sheep and have scattered us among the nations.
You sold your people for a pittance, gaining nothing from their sale.
You have made us a reproach to our neighbors, the scorn and derision of those around us.
You have made us a byword among the nations; the people shake their heads at us.
My disgrace is before me all day long, and my face is covered with shame
at the taunts of those who reproach and revile me,
because of the enemy, who is bent on revenge.
All this happened to us, though we had not forgotten you or been false to your covenant.
Our hearts had not turned back; our feet had not strayed from your path.
But you crushed us and made us a haunt for jackals and covered us over with deep darkness.
If we had forgotten the name of our God or spread out our hands to a foreign god,
would not God have discovered it, since he knows the secrets of the heart?
Yet for your sake we face death all day long; we are considered as sheep to be slaughtered.
Awake, O Lord! Why do you sleep? Rouse yourself! Do not reject us forever.
Why do you hide your face and forget our misery and oppression?
We are brought down to the dust; our bodies cling to the ground.
Rise up and help us; redeem us because of your unfailing love.

Little did I dream when I committed myself to you, Lord, that it would be the beginning of temptations, afflictions, and a precarious path leading through obscurity. Many of my companions have turned back or grown bitter. I cling to a thread of hope and wait for your help.

The Glory of a King who Trusts in the Lord

My heart is stirred by a noble theme as I recite my verses for the king; my tongue is the pen of a skillful writer.
You are the most excellent of men and your lips have been anointed with grace, since God has blessed you forever.
Gird your sword upon your side, O mighty one; clothe yourself with splendor and majesty.
In your majesty ride forth victoriously in behalf of truth, humility and righteousness; let your right hand display awesome deeds.
Let your sharp arrows pierce the hearts of the king's enemies; let the nations fall beneath your feet.
Your throne, O God, will last for ever and ever; a scepter of justice will be the scepter of your kingdom.
Your love righteousness and hate wickedness; therefore God, your God, has set you above your companions by anointing you with the oil of joy.
All your robes are fragrant with myrrh and aloes and cassia; from palaces adorned with ivory the music of the strings makes you glad.
Daughters of kings are among your honored women; at your right hand is the royal bride in gold of Ophir.
Listen, O daughter, consider and give ear: Forget your people and your father's house.
The king is enthralled by your beauty; honor him, for he is your lord.
The Daughter of Tyre will come with a gift, men of wealth will seek your favor.
All glorious is the princess within her chamber; her gown is interwoven with gold.
In embroidered garments she is led to the king; her virgin companions follow her and are brought to you.
They are led in with joy and gladness; they enter the palace of the king.
Your sons will take the place of your fathers; you will make them princes throughout the land.
I will perpetuate your memory through all generations; therefore the nations will praise you for ever and ever.

One day the church will enter into the glory of her Bridegroom and King, and into his holy joy. One day her offspring will rule over the nations inspiring worship and praise for the Lord. Together, their reign shall be characterized by grace.

He lifted me out of the slimy pit,
out of the mud and mire; he set my feet on
a rock and gave me a firm place to stand. He put a
new song in my mouth, a hymn
of praise to our God.
Ps.40:2-3

Lord of the Elements

*Be still, and know that I am God; I will be exalted
among the nations, I will be exalted in the earth.*

God is our refuge and strength, an ever present help in
trouble.
Therefore we will not fear, though the earth give way
and the mountains fall into the heart of the sea,
though its waters roar and foam and the mountains
quake with their surging. — Selah.
There is a river whose streams make glad the city of
God, the holy place where the Most High dwells.
God is within her, she will not fall; God will help her at
break of day.
Nations are in uproar, kingdoms fall; he lifts his voice,
the earth melts.
The Lord Almighty is with us; the God of Jacob is our
fortress. — Selah.
Come and see the works of the Lord, the desolations he
has brought on the earth.
He makes wars cease to the ends of the earth; he breaks
the bow and shatters the spear, he burns the shields with
fire.
»Be still, and know that I am God; I will be exalted
among the nations, I will be exalted in the earth.«
The Lord Almighty is with us; the God of Jacob is our
fortress. — Selah.

*The threats and rumors of war disturb our peace
of mind and fill children with fear. Natural
catastrophies continue to occur regularly
around the world. Our planet seems to writhe in
misery. How comforting to know it is but the
birthing-pains for a new world where the Lord is
the center. From his throne will flow a river of
joy which will heal the nations. His face will be
our shining sun, illuminating the whys of our*

The Lord of All Nations

*The nobles of the nations assemble as the people
of the God of Abraham, for the kings of the earth
belong to God; he is greatly exalted.*

Clap your hands, all you nations; shout to God with
cries of joy.
How awesome is the Lord Most High, the great King
over all the earth!
He subdued nations under us, peoples under our feet.
He chose our inheritance for us, the pride of Jacob,
whom he loved. — Selah.
God has ascended amid shouts of joy, the Lord amid the
sounding of trumpets.
Sing praises to God, sing praises; sing praises to our
King, sing praises.
For God is the King of all the earth; sing to him a psalm
of praise.
God reigns over the nations; God is seated on his holy
throne.
The nobles of the nations assemble as the people of the
God of Abraham, for the kings of the earth belong to
God; he is greatly exalted.

*Princes shall become as children, clapping and
shouting in exuberance for you, Lord. Children
shall gather together, spontaneously singing
praises before your throne. Hosannas will ring,
and I will join them!*

The City of the Lord

For this God is our God for ever and ever; he will be our guide even to the end.

Great is the Lord, and most worthy of praise, in the city of our God, his holy mountain. It is beautiful in its loftiness, the joy of the whole earth. Like the utmost heights of Zaphon is Mount Zion, the city of the Great King.
God is in her citadels; he has shown himself to be her fortress.

When the kings joined forces, when they advanced together,
they saw her and were astounded; they fled in terror. Trembling seized them there, pain like that of a woman in labor.
You destroyed them like ships of Tarshish shattered by an east wind.

As we have heard, so have we seen in the city of the Lord almighty, in the city of our God: God makes her secure forever. — Selah.

Within your temple, O God, we meditate on your unfailing love.
Like your name, O God, your praise reaches to the ends of the earth; your right hand is filled with righteousness. Mount Zion rejoices, the villages of Judah are glad because of your judgments.

Walk about Zion, go around her, count her towers, consider well her ramparts, view her citadels, that you may talk of them to the next generation.
For this God is our God for ever and ever; he will be our guide even to the end.

I walk about Zion and recount the times her towers have been my refuge, her bulwarks my defense, her palacial chambers, the sanctum for the King and I. Lord, I am a pilgrim on earth, not at home anywhere but in Zion.

Trust the Lord, Not Your Riches

My mouth will speak words of wisdom; the utterance frommy heart will give understanding.

Hear this, all you peoples; listen, all who live in this world, both low and high, rich and poor alike:
My mouth will speak words of wisdom; the utterance from my heart will give understanding.
I will turn my ear to a proverb; with the harp I will expound my riddle:
Why should I fear when evil days come, when wicked deceivers surround me —
those who trust in their wealth and boast of their great riches?
No man can redeem the life of another or give to God a ransom for him —
the ransom for a life is costly, no payment is ever enough
— that he should live on forever and not see decay.
For all can see that wise men die; the foolish and the senseless alike perish and leave their wealth to others.
Their tombs will remain their houses forever, their dwellings for endless generations, though they had named lands after themselves.
But man, despite his riches, does not endure; he is like the beasts that perish.
This is the fate of those who trust in themselves, and of their followers, who approve their sayings. — Selah.
Like sheep they are destined for the grave, and death will feed on them. The upright will rule over them in the morning; their forms will decay in the grave, far from their princely mansions.
But God will redeem my soul from the grave; he will surely take me to himself. — Selah.
Do not be overawed when a man grows rich, when the splendor of his house increases;
for he will take nothing with him when he dies, his splendor will not descend with him.
Though while he lived he counted himself blessed —
he will join the generation of his fathers, who will never see the light of life.
A man who has riches without understanding is like the beasts that perish.

Sin and death are towering equalizers of mankind. Redemption is the heart of the matter, and has been paid with the blood of God's lamb. My choice has been made to trust in his redemption and feed upon eternal things instead of establishing a life in the temporal.

The Lord Delights in Thank Offerings

The Mighty One, God, the Lord, speaks and summons the earth from the rising of the sun to the place where it sets.
From Zion, perfect in beauty, God shines forth.
Our God comes and will not be silent; a fire devours before him, and around him a tempest rages.
He summons the heavens above, and the earth, that he may judge his people:
»Gather to me my consercrated ones, who made a covenant with me by sacrifice.«
And the heavens proclaim his righteousness, for God himself is judge.
— Selah.
»Hear, O my people, and I will speak, O Israel, and I will testify against you: I am God, your God.
I do not rebuke you for your sacrifies or your burnt offerings, which are ever before me.
I have no need of a bull from your stall or of goats from your pens,
for every animal of the forest is mine, and the cattle on a thousand hills.
I know every bird in the mountains, and the creatures of the field are mine.
If I were hungry I would not tell you, for the world is mine, and all that is in it.
Do I eat the flesh of bulls or drink the blood of goats?
Sacrifice thank offerings to God, fulfill your vows to the Most High,
and call upon me in the day of trouble; I will deliver you, and you will honor me.«
But to the wicked, God says:
What right have you to recite my laws or take my covenant on your lips?
You hate my instruction and cast my words behind you.
When you see a thief, you join with him; you throw in your lot with adulterers.
You use your mouth for evil and harness your tongue to deceit.
Your speak continually against your brother and slander your own mother's son.
These things you have done and I kept silent; you thought I was altogether like you. But I will rebuke you and accuse you to your face.
»Consider this, you who forget God, or I will tear you to pieces, with none to rescue:
He who sacrifices thank offerings honors me, and he prepares the way so that I may show him the salvation of God.«

God will shine forth, and when he does we will see things from a new perspective. The fire of his holiness will burn away the haze through which we are used to looking.

The Lord Renews Your Spirit

Restore to me the joy of your salvation and grant me a willing spirit, to sustain me.

Have mercy on me, O God, according to your unfailing love; according to your great compassion blot out my transgressions.
Wash away all my iniquity and cleanse me from my sin.
For I know my transgressions, and my sin is always before me.
Against you, you only, have I sinned and done what is evil in your sight, so that you are proved right when you speak and justified when you judge.
Surely I have been a sinner from birth, sinful from the time my mother conceived me.
Surely you desire truth in the inner parts; you teach me wisdom in the inmost place.
Cleanse me with hyssop, and I will be clean; wash me, and I will be whiter than snow.
Let me hear joy and gladness; let the bones you have crushed rejoice.
Hide your face from my sins and blot out all my iniquity.
Create in me a pure heart, O God, and renew a steadfast spirit within me.
Do not cast me from your presence or take your Holy Spirit from me.
Restore to me the joy of your salvation and grant me a willing spirit, to sustain me.
Then I will teach transgressors your ways, and sinners will turn back to you.
Save me from bloodguilt, O God, the God who saves me, and my tongue will sing of your righteousness.
O Lord, open my lips, and my mouth will declare your praise.
You do not delight in sacrifice, or I would bring it; you do not take pleasure in burnt offerings.
The sacrifices of God are a broken spirit; a broken and contrite heart, O God, you will not despise.
In your good pleasure make Zion prosper; build up the walls of Jerusalem.
Then there will be righteous sacrifices, whole burnt offerings to delight you; then bulls will be offered on your altar.

Lord, you did not turn away in dismay at my broken life, but entered it and got involved. You covered my sin with a blanket of forgiveness, cleansed me of guilt and began to mend my fragmented spirit.

Trust God's Unfailing Love

I will praise you forever for what you have done; in your name I will hope, for your name is good.

Why do you boast of evil, you mighty man? Why do you boast all day long, you who are a disgrace in the eyes of God?
Your tongue plots destruction; it is like a sharpened razor, you who practice deceit.
You love evil rather than good, falsehood rather than speaking the truth. — Selah.
You love every harmful word, O you deceitful tongue!

Surely God will bring you down to everlasting ruin: He will snatch you up and tear you from your tent; he will uproot you from the land of the living. — Selah.
The righteous will see and fear; they will laugh at him, saying,
»Here now is the man who did not make God his stronghold but trusted in his great wealth and grew strong by destroying others!«

But I am like an olive tree flourishing in the house of God; I trust in God's unfailing love for ever and ever.
I will praise you forever for what you have done; in your name I will hope, for your name is good. I will praise you in the presence of your saints.

The wicked and the wealthy bloom alongside each other here on earth. Both assume independence from God. The wind blows — their blossoms disintegrate and drift away. God's goodness is eternally in season!

Therefore we will not fear, though the earth
give way and the mountains fall into the heart of the sea, though its waters roar and
foam and the mountains quake with their surging.
Ps.46:2-3

The Wise Man Seeks God

The fool says in his heart, »There is no God.«

The fool says in his heart, »There is no God.« They are corrupt, and their ways are vile; there is no one who does good.

God looks down from heaven on the sons of men to see if there are any who understand, any who seek God. Everyone has turned away, they have together become corrupt; there is no one who does good, not even one.

Will the evildoers never learn — those who devour my people as men eat bread and who do not call on God? There they were, overwhelmed with dread, where there was nothing to dread. God scattered the bones of those who attacked you; you put them to shame, for God despised them.

Oh, that salvation for Israel would come out of Zion! When God restores the fortunes of his people, let Jacob rejoice and Israel be glad!

Lord, how often we, your own people, take you for granted. We trust you for our eternal salvation, but allow our life styles to merge with those of the foolish. We are in captivity to our own will. When will we understand your heart, your need for true trust and total committment?

Call to God, and He Will Save You

O God; listen to the words of my mouth.

Save me, O God, by your name; vindicate me by your might.
Hear my prayer, O God; listen to the words of my mouth.
Strangers are attacking me; ruthless men seek my life — men without regard for God. — Selah.
Surely God is my help; the Lord is the one who sustains me.
Let evil recoil on those who slander me; in your faithfulness destroy them.
I will sacrifice a freewill offering to you; I will praise your name, O Lord, for it is good.
For he has delivered me from all my troubles, and my eyes have looked in triumph on my foes.

Sometimes we must rise up through praise and leave the backside of the mountain in order to see the light of God breaking through the clouds. We must live on the bright side. The world calls it optimism but we know it as faith, based on the solid word of God.

My Place of Shelter

I said, »Oh, that I had the wings of a dove! I would fly away and be at rest — I would flee far away and stay in the desert; — Selah.

Listen to my prayer, O God, do not ignore my plea; hear me and answer me. My thoughts trouble me and I am distraught at the voice of the enemy, at the stares of the wicked; for they bring down suffering upon me and revile me in their anger.

My heart is in anguish within me; the terrors of death assail me.
Fear and trembling have beset me; horror has overwhelmed me.
I said, »Oh, that I had the wings of a dove! I would fly away and be at rest —
I would flee far away and stay in the desert;
I would hurry to my place of shelter, far from the tempest and storm.«

Confuse the wicked, O Lord, confound their speech, for I see violence and strife in the city.
Day and night they prowl about on its walls; malice and abuse are within it.
Destructive forces are at work in the city; threats and lies never leave its streets.

If an enemy were insulting me, I could endure it; if a foe were raising himself against me, I could hide from him.
But it is you, a man like myself, my companion, my close friend,
with whom I once enjoyed sweet fellowship as we walked with the throng at the house of God.

My expectations were too high, Lord. The sweet springs have become bitter. Disillusionment and destruction have wounded my will to carry on. I will hide in the cleft of the rock, in the secret place of the stairs until you woo me forth again to flight.

Call to God, and He Saves You

But I call to God, and the Lord saves me. Evening, morning and noon I cry out in distress, and he hears my voice.

Let death take my enemies by surprise; let them go down alive to the grave, for evil finds lodging among them.
But I call to God, and the Lord saves me.
Evening, morning and noon I cry out in distress, and he hears my voice.
He ransoms me unharmed from the battle waged against me, even though many oppose me.
God, who is enthroned forever, will hear them and afflict them — Selah — men who never change their ways and have no fear of God.
My companion attacks his friends; he violates his covenant.
His speech is smooth as butter, yet war is in his heart; his words are more soothing than oil, yet they are drawn swords.

Peace in my soul is more important than victory in my battles. Make of my soul a garden, Lord, where I can find comfort to assuage the torture of sharp words and hostile affronts. I turn to you to restore what has been lost.

What Can Man Do To Me?

My enemies will turn back when I call for help. By this I will know that God is for me.

Be merciful to me, O God, for men hotly pursue me; all day long they press their attack.
My slanderers pursue me all day long; many are attacking me in their pride.
When I am afraid, I will trust in you.
In God, whose word I praise, in God I trust; I will not be afraid. What can mortal man do to me?
All day long they twist my words; they are always plotting to harm me.
They conspire, they lurk, they watch my steps, eager to take my life.
On no account let them escape; in your anger, O God, bring down the nations.
Record my lament; list my tears on your scroll — are they not in your record?
Then my enemies will turn back when I call for help. By this I will know that God is for me.
In God, whose word I praise, in the Lord, whose word I praise —
in God I trust; I will not be afraid. What can man do to me?
I am under vows to you, O God; I will present my thank offerings to you.
For you have delivered my soul from death and my feet from stumbling, that I may walk before God in the light of life.

Like David, my life has its share of detours, backtracking, and tears. Yet not one step is wasted, nor is one tear cried in vain. For you treasure each of them, Lord. You regard them as eternity's riches.

Be Exalted O God

Great is your love, reaching to the heavens; your faithfulness reaches to the skies.

Have mercy on me, O God, have mercy on me, for in you my soul takes refuge. I will take refuge in the shadow of your wings until the disaster has passed.

I cry out to God Most High, to God, who fulfills his purpose for me.

He sends from heaven and saves me, rebuking those who hotly pursue me; — Selah — God sends his love and his faithfulness.

I am in the midst of lions; I lie among ravenous beasts — men whose teeth are spears and arrows, whose tongues are sharp swords.

Be exalted, O God, above the heavens; let your glory be over all the earth.

They spread a net for my feet — I was bowed down in distress. They dug a pit in my path — but they have fallen into it themselves. — Selah.

My heart is steadfast, O God, my heart is steadfast; I will sing and make music.

Awake, my soul! Awake, harp and lyre! I will awaken the dawn.

I will praise you , O Lord, among the nations; I will sing of you among peoples.

For great is your love, reaching to the heavens; your faithfulness reaches to the skies.

Be exalted, O God, above the heavens; let your glory be over all the earth.

I can depend on the one who creates for me new beginnings, who makes a masterpiece of each design. When I am threatened with destruction or harm, he hovers around. The shadows that I see are merely evidence of his sheltering wings.

The Lord Judges Righteously

Then men will say, »Surely the righteous still are rewarded; surely there is a God who judges the earth.«

Do you rulers indeed speak justly? Do you judge uprightly among men?
No, in your heart you devise injustice, and your hands mete out violence on the earth.
Even from birth the wicked go astray; from the womb they are wayward and speak lies.
Their venom is like the venom of a snake, like that of a cobra that has stopped its ears,
that will not heed the tune of the charmer, however skillful the enchanter may be.

Break the teeth in their mouths, O God; tear out, O Lord, the fangs of the lions!
Let them vanish like water that flows away; when they draw the bow, let their arrows be blunted.
Like a slug melting away as it moves along, like a stillborn child, may they not see the sun.

Before your pots can feel the heat of the thorns — whether they be green or dry — the wicked will be swept away.
The righteous will be glad when they are avenged, when they bathe their feet in the blood of the wicked.
Then men will say, »Surely the righteous still are rewarded; surely there is a God who judges the earth.

One day your judgement will flow crystal clear, Lord. You will allow mankind his final choice. You will allow wickedness to reach its climax. How much better for the wicked to fall under the vengence of mortals than under your vengence when the moment of reckoning arrives.

I will praise you, O Lord, among the nations;
I will sing of you among the peoples. For great is your love,
reaching to the heavens; your faithfulness reaches to the skies.
Be exalted, O God, above the heavens; let
your glory be over all the earth.
Ps.57:9-11

The Lord, Our Shield

You are my fortress, my refuge in times of trouble.

Deliver me from my enemies, O God; protect me from those who rise up against me.
Deliver me from evildoers and save me from bloodthirsty men.
See how they lie in wait for me! Fierce men conspire against me for no offense or sin of mine, O Lord.
I have done no wrong, yet they are ready to attack me. Arise to help me; look on my plight!
O Lord God Almighty, the God og Israel, rouse yourself to punish all the nations; show no mercy to wicked traitors. — Selah.
They return at evening, snarling like dogs, and prowl about the city.
See what they spew from their mouths — they spew out swords from their lips, and they say, »Who can hear us?«
But you, O Lord, laugh at them; you scoff at all those nations.
O my Strength, I watch for you; you, O God, are my fortress, my loving God.
God will go before me and will let me gloat over those who slander me.
But do not kill them, O Lord our shield, or my people will forget. In your might make them wander about, and bring them down.
For the sins of their mouths, for the words of their lips, let them be caught in their pride. For the curses and lies they utter,
consume them in wrath, consume them till they are no more. Then it will be known to the ends of the earth that God rules over Jacob. — Selah.
They return at evening, snarling like dogs, and prowl about the city.
They wander about for food and howl if not satisfied.
But I will sing of your strength, in the morning I will sing of your love; for you are my fortress, my refuge in times of trouble.
O my Strength, I sing praise to you; you, O God, are my fortress, my loving God.

The security I depended upon has crumbled. All that remains is my song, the one you gave me so long ago. I will sing it day-in and day-out. My prayers will rise to you as the melody, my praise as the harmony. The song is powerful because it is of you.

You Have Been Angry - Now Restore Us

With God we will gain the victory, and he will trample down our enemies.

You have rejected us, O God, and burst forth upon us; you have been angry — now restore us!
You have shaken the land and torn it open; mend its fractures, for it is quaking.
You have shown your people desperate times; you have given us wine that makes us stagger.

But for those who fear you, you have raised a banner to be unfurled against the bow. — Selah.

Save us and help us with your right hand, that those you love may be delivered.
God has spoken from his sanctuary: »In triumph I will parcel out Shechem and measure off the Valley of Succoth.
Gilead is mine, and Manasseh is mine; Ephraim is my helmet, Judah my scepter.
Moab is my washbasin, upon Edom I toss my sandal; over Philistia I shout in triumph.«

Who will bring me to the fortified city? Who will lead me to Edom?
Is it not you, O God, you who have rejected us and no longer go out with our armies?
Give us aid against the enemy, for the help of man is worthless.
With God we will gain the victory, and he will trample down our enemies.

Lord, you arise in your authority and pronounce that you will conquer. You admonish those who trust you to display the banner of your might and love. You rejoice because of the truth. No matter how contradictory the evidence, you are in control. You will have the final word.

In the Shelter of Your Wings

*I long to dwell in your tent forever and take refuge in the
shelter of your wings. — Selah.*

Hear my cry, O God; listen to my prayer.
From the ends of the earth I call to you, I call as my
heart grows faint; lead me to the rock that is higher than
I

For you have been my refuge, a strong tower against the
foe.
I long to dwell in your tent forever and take refuge in
the shelter of your wings. — Selah.
For you have heard my vows, O God; you have given
me the heritage of those who fear your name.

Increase the days of the king's life, his yeras for many
generations.
May he be enthroned in God's presence forever;
appoint your love and faithfulness to protect him.
Then will I ever sing praise to your name and fulfill my
vows day after day.

*Lord, I carry within myself a yearning to be part
of something that is bigger than myself. You
lead me to the end of the earth, to the limit of my
ability. You put before me a mountain and tell
me to climb it. Then I realize you are merely
answering the longings of my spirit. I look to
you for leadership and provision for the ascent.*

In God Alone...

My salvation and my honor depend on God.

My soul finds rest in God alone; my salvation comes
from him.
He alone is my rock and my salvation; he is my fortress,
I will never be shaken.

How long will you assault a man? Would all of you throw
him down — this leaning wall, this tottering fence?
They fully intend to topple him from his lofty place; they
take delight in lies. With their mouths they bless, but in
their hearts they curse. — Selah.

Find rest, O my soul, in God alone; my hope comes
from him.
He alone is my rock and my salvation; he is my fortress,
I will not be shaken.
My salvation and my honor depend on God; He is my
mighty rock, my refuge.
Trust in him at all times, O people; pour out your hearts
to him, for God is our refuge. — Selah.

Lowborn men are but a breath, the highborn are but a
lie; if weighed on a balance, they are nothing; together
they are only a breath.
Do not trust in extortion or take pride in stolen goods;
though your riches increase, do not set your heart on
them.

One thing God has spoken, two things have I heard:
that you, O God, are strong,
and that you, O Lord, are loving. Surely you will reward
each person according to what he has done.

*True wisdom is to put my expectation in God,
not passively but actively. Status, success and
wealth are illusions. Their lure is a lie. My
affections shall not be fettered to them, but to
the rock of my strength. He will dominate the
landscape of my life.*

I Stay Close to You

I think of you through the watches of the night. Because you are my help, I sing in the shadow of your wings. I stay close to you; your right hand upholds me.

O God, you are my God, earnestly I seek you; my soul thirsts for you, my body longs for you, in a dry and weary land where there is no water.

I have seen you in the sanctuary and beheld your power and your glory.

Because your love is better than life, my lips will glorify you.

I will praise you as long as I live, and in your name I will lift up my hands.

My soul will be satisfied as with the richest of foods; with singing lips my mouth will praise you.

On my bed I remember you; I think of you through the watches of the night.

Because you are my help, I sing in the shadow of your wings.

I stay close to you; your right hand upholds me.

They who seek my life will be destroyed; they will be given over to the sword and become food for jackals.

But the king will rejoice in God; all who swear by God's name will praise him, while the mouths of liars will be silenced.

Lord, if I do not get an early start on seeking you I may find that it is too late. Like the Sahara, my life will be inflicted with a cycle of drought reinforcing drought if I do not keep my resources in balance. I must plant an abundance of praise, meditation and fellowship in order to protect and secure a green and thriving life of righteousness.

Lord, Protect Me!

*Let the righteous rejoice in the Lord and take refuge in
him; let all the upright in heart praise him!*

Hear me, O God, as I voice my complaint; protect my
life from the threat of the enemy.
Hide me from the conspiracy of the wicked, from that
noisy crowd of evildoers,
who sharpen their tongues like swords and aim their
words like deadly arrows.
They shoot from ambush at the innocent man; they
shoot at him suddenly, without fear.
They encourage each other in evil plans, they talk about
hiding their snares; they say, »Who will see them?«
They plot injustice and say, »We have devised a perfect
plan!« Surely the mind and heart of man are cunning.
But God will shoot them with arrows; suddenly they will
be struck down.
He will turn their own tongues against them and bring
them to ruin; all who see them will shake their heads in
scorn.
All mankind will fear; they will proclaim the works of
God and ponder what he has done.
Let the righteous rejoice in the Lord and take refuge in
him; let all the upright in heart praise him!

*Preserve our life from fear, Lord. It is hard
enough to bear the fact that nothing can
eliminate the great sorrows from our lives. But
let us rob them of their sting with faith, and
smother their small, daily counterparts with
softened hearts. Let us spill our pearls of
laughter across their path. We need protection
from the secret intentions of the wicked. But we
need equal protection from paralysing fears,
fears that would take the sparkle out of our
sence of wonder.*

A God of Abundance

You care for the land and water it; you enrich it abundantly. The streams of God are filled with water to provide the people with grain, for so you have ordained it.

Praise awaits you, O God, in Zion; to you our vows will be fulfilled.
O you who hear prayer, to you all men will come.
When we were overwhelmed by sins, you atoned for our transgressions.
Blessed is the man you choose and bring near to live in your courts! We are filled with the good things of your house, of your holy temple.

You answer us with awesome deeds of righteousness, O God our Savior, the hope of all the ends of the earth and of the farthest seas,
who formed the mountains by your power, having armed yourself with strength,
who stilled the roaring of the nations.
Those living far away fear your wonders; where morning dawns and evening fades you call forth songs of joy.

You care for the land and water it; you enrich it abundantly. The streams of God are filled with water to provide the people with grain, for so you have ordained it.
You drench its furrows and level its ridges; you soften it with showers and bless its crops.
You crown the year with your bounty, and your carts overflow with abundance.
The grasslands of the desert overflow; the hills are clothed with gladness.
The meadows are covered with grain; they shout for joy and sing.

You make the tides rejoice. The embankments along the shores hear the praise and join the song. As for me, I am flesh and bone and sinful of nature, but I hear the music of creation, am led to repent and receive atonement. You chose me. Hallelujah!

You care for the land
and water it; you enrich it abundantly.
The streams of God are filled with water
to provide the people with grain,
for so you have ordained it.
Ps.65:9

Praise Him!

Praise our God, O peoples, let the sound of his praise be heard; he has preserved our lives and kept our feet from slipping.

Shout with joy to God, all the earth!
Sing to the glory of his name; offer him glory and praise!
Say to God, »How awesome are your deeds! So great is your power that your enemies cringe before you.
All the earth bows down to you; they sing praise to you, they sing praise to your name.« — Selah.

Come and see what God has done, how awesome his works in man's behalf!
He turned the sea into dry land, they passed through the river on foot — come, let us rejoice in him.
He rules forever by his power, his eyes watch the nations — let not the rebellious rise up against him. — Selah.

Praise our God, O peoples, let the sound of his praise be heard;
he has preserved our lives and kept our feet from slipping.
For you, O God, tested us; you refined us like silver.
You brought us into prison and laid burdens on our backs.
You let men ride over our heads; we went through fire and water, but you brought us to a place of abundance.

Where would I be, Lord, if you had not exposed me to the elements of affliction, nor dared to begin the refining process? How hollow and how empty my praise would ring. I had my share of miracles when passing through the waters. But the greatest miracle of all is that you knew when to step back and allow the miracle to be produced within me. Rich fulfillment is not a state of outward circumstance but the transformation of my spirit.

Praise Him!

Come and listen, all you who fear God; let me tell you what he has done for me.

I will come to your temple with burnt offerings and
fulfill my vows to you —
vows my lips promised and my mouth spoke when I was
in trouble.
I will sacrifice fat animals to you and an offering of rams;
I will offer bulls and goats. — Selah.
Come and listen, all you who fear God; let me tell you
what he has done for me.
I cried out to him with my mouth; his praise was on my
tongue.
If I had cherished sin in my heart, the Lord would not
have listened;
but God has surely listened and heard my voice in
prayer.
Praise be to God, who has not rejected my prayer or
withheld his love from me!

*How marvelous, Lord, to contemplate the
expanse of your mercy towards individuals. To
each man and woman in history you offer this
treasure of intimate fellowship and answered
prayer. You have even provided the offering
required: the blood of Christ, a river of love
joining our deep-rooted needs to your abundant
seas.*

Benediction

God will bless us, and all the ends of the earth will fear him.

May God be gracious to us and bless us and make his face shine upon us; — Selah
may your ways be known on earth, your salvation among all nations.
May the peoples praise you, O God; may all the peoples praise you.
May the nations be glad and sing for joy, for you rule the peoples justly and guide the nations of the earth. — Selah.
May the peoples praise you, O God; may all the peoples praise you.
Then the land will yield its harvest, and God, our God, will bless us.
God will bless us, and all the ends of the earth will fear him.

Lord, do bless us; not so we can bask in the glow of your favor, but so that we have resources with which to share your way of salvation. Cause your face to shine upon us that we may pass it along to all nations. Peace on earth will follow, again the earth will yield its increase, and You

Find rest, O my soul, in God alone; my hope comes from him.
He alone is my rock and my salvation; he is my fortress, I shall not be shaken.
My salvation and my honour depend on God; he is my mighty rock, my refuge.
Trust in him at all times, O people; pour out your hearts
to him, for God is our refuge.
Ps.62:5-8

I will praise you, O Lord, among the nations;
I will sing of you among the peoples. For great is your love,
reaching to the heavens; your faithfulness reaches to the skies.
Be exalted, O God, above the heavens; let
your glory be over all the earth.
Ps.57:9-11